please shine down on me.

Oh Mister Sun, Sun,
Mister Golden Sun,

THE ORIGINAL
INDESTRUCTIBLES®
Chew Proof • Rip Proof • Nontoxic • 100% Washable
MISTER GOLDEN SUN
MILLIONS OF COPIES SOLD!
BECKY PAIGE

Oh Mister Sun, Sun,
Mister Golden Sun,

hiding behind a tree.

These little children are asking you

to please come out so
we can play with you.

Oh Mister Sun, Sun,
Mister Golden Sun,

please shine down on me.

Shine down
on me,

shine, shine, shine!

THE ORIGINAL INDESTRUCTIBLES®

For ages 0 and up!

Books babies can really sink their gums into!

Oh Mister Sun, Sun, Mister Golden Sun, please shine down on me!

Read and sing the beloved song with baby in a book that's INDESTRUCTIBLE.

DEAR PARENTS: INDESTRUCTIBLES are built for the way babies "read": with their hands and mouths. INDESTRUCTIBLES won't rip or tear and are 100% washable. They're made for baby to hold, grab, chew, pull, and bend.

CHEW ALL THESE AND MORE!

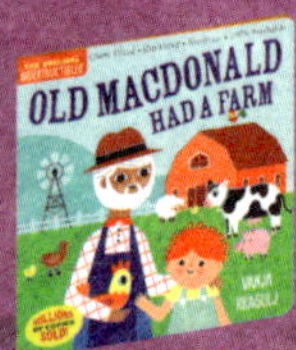

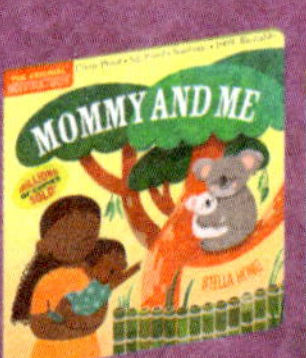

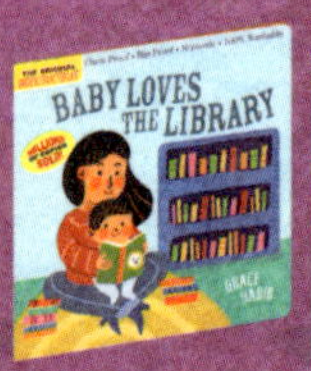

$5.99 US / $7.99 Can.
ISBN 978-1-5235-3431-9
50599
9 781523 534319

 Library of Congress Cataloging-in-Publication Data is available. Workman Kids is an imprint of Workman Publishing, a division of Hachette Book Group, Inc.

Distributed in the United Kingdom by Hachette UK Ltd., Carmelite House, 50 Victoria Embankment, London EC4Y 0DZ. Distributed in Europe by Hachette Livre, 58 rue Jean Bleuzen, 92 178 Vanves Cedex, France.
Contact special.markets@hbgusa.com regarding special discounts for bulk purchases.

First Edition April 2026 | 10 9 8 7 6 5 4 3 2 1
Printed in Shenzhen, China 01/26 | IMFP

WORKMAN PUBLISHING • Hachette Book Group, Inc., 1290 Avenue of the Americas, New York, NY 10104 • indestructiblesinc.com